I dedicate this first book to

Kitty,

my beloved Mother,

whose prayers and unconditional love,

brought me to the feet of

"Jesus",
my Lord and Savior.

ACKNOWLEDGMENTS

To Most Reverend Bishop Sam Jacobs who without even being aware of it, "sealed my commission to write this book, as he preached under the conviction and inspiration of the Holy Spirit," during the 1992 Wildwood Charismatic Conference (Saturday afternoon session).

To my family and friends who believed and prayed for this work . . . especially Warren, Doris, Syl, Jan and Don.

To Jimmy and our children who first recognized this gift in me and through their love and encouragement gave me the **desire** to write.

To Eileen, my cousin, confidante and companion for providing me with a **vision** and a **haven**.

God bless **you**, Ruth, (and your computer), for turning this **work** into a **reality**.

WITH SPECIAL ACKNOWLEDGMENT

To Ed, my husband, my friend, my love. Thank you for your **love** and **support**, for giving me the **motivation** I needed, by helping me realize these words were **medicine** for a world in need of healing . . .

Contents

INTRODUCTION

Although this is a small book, I believe I have captured man's search for inner peace, self confidence and the truth that we are all one by race, the human race.

I write simply, as one who has experienced the empowerment of our God. Call Him by whatever name you like. He is our creator. He sent His son to save us and His Spirit to help us. It is my hope that this book can help you not only to follow your dreams but to fulfill your dreams as you grow in faith, hope and love.

This book is grounded on faith, conviction and experience. It was written for those who do not know the Lord, for those who are in the mainstream Church and want a deeper personal relationship with their God and lastly, to encourage all those who are on a spiritual journey.

1

Now it begins . . .

PREFACE

As I sit alone by the ocean, on this magnificent October afternoon, I **know** that I have come, Lord, to commit this book into your hands. It was here, fourteen years ago, that you first spoke to my heart and asked me to write for your honor and glory.

Although I never **answered** your **call**, these words never left my heart:

*"I have commissioned you. Take the **power** of the sword, my **word**, which I have **hidden** in your heart, and **proclaim** it. Let the **written** word take root in the hearts of my people, so that my **word will** become flesh in **them**, that they may live . . . and move . . . and have their **being** . . . in me."*

Since I have completed only eight years of school and know absolutely nothing about creative writing, I ask, "How can this be, Lord?" He answers, *"Not by education, nor by skill, but by my Spirit, you shall write."* So today I have come to say your word shall not return to you **void.** "Here I am Lord; send me. Send me, wherever you want me to go, to proclaim the Good News. Please bless and anoint this **written** word and all those who **read it.**"

To God be the glory!

THE WORD OF THE LORD

For I am the Lord your God who grasps your right hand.
It is I, who say to you, fear not, I will help you.

Isaiah 41, 13.

Although I did not fully understand the meaning of that word as I read it almost twenty years ago, I **know** it was the spark that ignited something deep inside me **to** write. I started to write poems, prayers and songs telling "Jesus" of my love for him.

All were my love letters **to** "Jesus", for Him alone, never dreaming I would one day write a book **for** "Jesus".

I have since come to understand that **gentle** touch of God. I know now he was molding me, transforming me to do the work for which I was **sent** into the world to do: glorify His name throughout the earth.

His name is "Jesus," the "Christ."

He is the **Son** of the **Living** God.

His **Holy Spirit** enables us to cry out, "Abba Father!"

4

OUR FATHER, WHO ART IN HEAVEN . . .

I'd like to talk to you about our Father. He formed me before I was born, while I was still in the womb. The Father who called me by name, *"Kathleen, you are mine."* He saw that I would be **imperfect**. He saw that I would cause Him **pain** and **suffering** "through my **indifference**." He knew all about the **medical bills** I would incur. He even knew he would have to provide for "one **more** child." Oh yes, there would certainly be a generation gap and a **life long** process of misunderstandings and lack of communication. How could He **still** call me into being? Because I was "**conceived** in His mind" and He fell in love with the "thought" of me. So much so, He decided to **form** me with His own hands. Just the way **He** wanted me to be. Perhaps not the way I would one day **want** to be, but just the same, created in **His** "likeness and image."

As He **breathed life** into me, His thought became **flesh** in my mother's womb. Looking at me as I was being formed in secret, He **sighed** with love and spoke a word of "mission and purpose" to my heart. *"You were created to know me, to love me and to serve me and indeed your heart shall not rest **unless** it rests **in Me**."*

6

IS "YOUR" HEART RESTLESS

Let me tell you about our brother, "Jesus."

You may have heard of Him being referred to as Wonderful, Counselor, the Morning Star or perhaps, the Prince of Peace. I can attest to this personally, as He has been a **wonderful counselor** to me, guiding me, leading me, making straight my crooked paths. Thank you Jesus. In the dark times of my life, His glorious light rose up within me like a **morning star** and **dispelled** the darkness. Thank you Jesus.

In Isaiah, God tells us He will keep in perfect peace those who keep their mind and heart **set** on Him. He certainly has fulfilled that word in my life. For He has been my **peace** in the midst of turmoil, my **joy** in the deepest of sorrow, my **hope** in times of uncertainty.

I have twelve wonderful children and while I was still nursing our last, my husband was diagnosed with colon cancer. The doctor's news devastated everyone. We had such a beautiful relationship, twelve beautiful children and so many dreams yet to be fulfilled. Ten months later

Jimmy was gone. I can only tell you, that those ten months were a sacred time, a time filled with a peace that went beyond all understanding.

One night, shortly after Jimmy died, I found my little boy Brian staring out the window. "How long will Daddy be gone?", he asked. My heart actually ached and my eyes filled with tears as I answered, "Forever, Brian. You know Daddy is in Heaven now, but He will always live in our hearts and he'll always love you. Being only five at the time, Brian pressed me further, "How long is forever, Mommy?" I could not speak. How long is forever, indeed. I simply held him close to me and silently prayed for God to help us.

That evening Brian's words burned deep in my heart, "How long is forever, Mommy?" This little son that I loved so much, struck a cord within me; Jimmy was gone forever for me too! Lying in bed that night, I started to feel restless; though tired, I could not sleep. I got up out of bed, turned on the lights and started to read my bible. Putting the bible down, I started to cry. I longed to hear Jim's voice, but only silence came. I remember saying out loud, "Oh Lord, if only I could hear his voice one more time."

At that very moment, the lights went out. Thinking the bulb blew, I tried to put another light on and realized all the lights were out. I found the flashlight and went down into the basement. Groping in the cluttered storage area, I found the breaker and flipped it on. Turning to leave, I saw a tape recorder on a table. I wondered, "What in the world is that doing here," and brought it back up with me.

I noticed a tape was inside of the recorder and decided to listen to it. When I pushed the play button, this is what I heard: "Hi ya honey, this is Jimmy." There was not the slightest doubt in my mind, that God heard my cry and answered me. Unbeknown to me, but not to the Lord, Jimmy was making a tape for me and the children, a message of love and trust in the Lord. From that moment on, my soul was at peace.

People marveled at my **strength**, when in fact, I had **none**. What they were seeing, was a courage born of hope, hope in the Lord.

So many people need peace and yet they can't seem to find it. They search for peace in many different ways and yet there is only **one** way!

HIS NAME IS "JESUS"

He truly is **the Way**. No **other** way will completely fulfill you, **once** and for **always.** There is no **love** that will last forever, save God's love. Mankind with all our technology and creativity cannot bring forth **lasting** peace or pleasure. **Only** the **Creator** and **His love** are from "everlasting to everlasting." All else is temporary. Haven't you found this to be true? Truth. He **alone** is the **truth.** He **alone** can and **will** set you free.

He will set you free to become who you really are— child of the **living** God. In Him there is **no** darkness at all. **Sin** is darkness. "Jesus" will speak the truth to your heart and break **any** and **every** bond that holds a child of God bound. There is **nothing** that will ever separate **you** from the love of God. Not drugs or alcohol. Not abortion, which **is** murder, nor immorality in all its **forms.** He wants us to turn away from all wrong doing and turn to

Him as He offers forgiveness through His unconditional love. **Everyone** who "seeks" forgiveness with a contrite heart will "receive" forgiveness.

Only you can **choose** life or death as they are put before you. I ask you to choose **life** and **live** . . .

I HAVE COME THAT YOU MAY HAVE LIFE
AND HAVE IT TO THE FULLEST. John 10, 10.

This is not **my** promise to you, but the promise of
"Jesus," by whose **name** every knee on earth, in heaven
and below the earth shall bend. His name is above **every**
other name, including cancer, anxiety, fear, doubt,
insecurity, incest, child abuse and any other name you
could imagine; which means **you** are **above**, and not
beneath, any other name.

If you feel burdened or **weighed down** by any name,
situation or circumstance in life, then you are **not**
receiving the **benefit** of **that promise**. I **know**, because
once **I** was blind, but now I see. I see, looking back over
my life, all the times I tried to "do it my way" and
failed—as a child, young adult and as a grown woman. I
remember thinking, Peggy Lee said it all, in the song, "Is
That All There Is?" Every day I got out of bed in the
morning, lived out the day and went back to bed at night.
I wasn't **unhappy** with my life; I guess you could say I
thought it was **status-quo**. I loved my husband and

children deeply and, I thought, even my God. Yet deep inside, I felt life was **monotonous**.

Until, July 15, 1972, on my 29th Birthday in St. Augustine , Florida. While vacationing and taking in the sights, I was drawn to a little Catholic Church named "Nombre Dios." As I entered the Church, I felt moved to kneel down and a gentle stirring began within me.

WHO TOUCHED ME . . .

It was a feeling I never remembered having, although I know now, it was God leaving His **imprint** on me. This began a quest for me to find out "who touched me." That was the beginning of **new life** for me.

Just the way we react to new life when admiring a new born, so too, God is with us. We are in awe and we're especially gentle, very tender, even quiet so as not to startle. That's how the Lord was with me. I couldn't quite **hear** Him. His **touch** was gentle and tender, almost elusive. Where was this God? How do you talk to Him? How do you reach out and touch Him back? How do you let Him know you want more? I started to go to Church, something I had not done in many years, not because I was supposed to, not because I wanted to set a good example for my young children, but simply because I **wanted** to. Wow!

I began to read the Bible, something I **never** did before. I never really **saw** one up close until I felt **moved** to go **buy** one. I can only tell you that as I read the Bible, His

word became **flesh** to me and I started to fall in love with my God, my Father, the one I had no recollection of, yet somehow knew I had bonded with before my world began. As I continued going to Mass and reading the Bible, I began to weep during Holy Communion. I wasn't sad; no, that wasn't the feeling. I was sorrowful to the depth of my heart, for the **indifference** I showed Him through the years. I felt as though my heart was actually breaking. I wanted Him to **know** I would **die** for Him if it would let Him know how much I loved Him. In my inmost being He whispered, *"I am breaking your heart of stone towards me. You say you would die for me. I only ask you to live for Me."*

During Holy Communion I felt the emptiness, the separation. I even felt like an outcast. I thought, "Others walk to receive you in Holy Communion and I must remain in my pew." (I was divorced and remarried outside the Church and therefore excommunicated from the Sacraments at the time.)

"Jesus" spoke to my heart . . . *"I have given you a taste of My suffering. When my children are not in communion with Me, I must remain standing at the door, knocking until they open the door of their heart to* *me. Be comforted in knowing I am sharing **My life** with you, Kathleen."*

I continued in conversation and companionship with "Jesus" throughout that year, growing more aware of His presence in my life. To my amazement, others often remarked, "There is something different about you. I can't put my finger on it; what is it? My faith, still so small, my character, still too weak, to acknowledge my God. What a poor witness I was!

But I was soon to be **filled** with the **power of His Spirit!**

AND WITH GREAT POWER
THE APOSTLES GAVE WITNESS TO THE
RESURRECTION OF THE LORD "JESUS". Acts 4, 33.

Quite by accident, or so I thought at the time, I found myself at a Charismatic prayer meeting. I had my mother with me that evening. We happened to walk in on "The Life in the Spirit Seminars," which, as we quickly found out, were asking for a seven week commitment, a commitment, I might add, we had no intention of keeping. Each week they would give a different talk about this so called life in the spirit. This evening's talk was to be on God's love. We decided to stay rather than get up and walk out at that point. Although my mother had not been to Mass, except for funerals and weddings, since I was a child, she had a deep love of God and she encouraged me to really listen to what was being said.

After the talk, everyone began to pray, hands uplifted, praising God for this and thanking God for that. Being a Catholic, I was a little unnerved by it. After all, Mass was so solemn, you just didn't speak out that way. I thought it was nice, but definitely **not** for me. As I swept the circle with my eyes, there was no doubt of the sincerity of the people. The freedom they had before the Lord was beautiful, but still, definitely **not** for me. As the meeting drew to a close, they started to sing another song, called, "Jesus Is Lord." As they continued to sing, the music touched me deeply and the words cut through my heart like a knife. I started to weep—not cry, but weep. I am not a person easily moved to tears. As a matter of fact, I am a very low key person. But all of a sudden, I was filled with a deep sorrow for walking away from the Church I loved so much as a child and for turning my back on my God who I had come to know and love. I was sorry for all the mistakes I had made, for every sin I ever committed, and I started to sob uncontrollably. When someone asked if I wanted to see the priest, I could only sob, "No, I am excommunicated." Unbeknown to me, the priest was waved over and I heard a strong but gentle voice, "Would you like me to pray with you?" I could only continue to say, and not very audibly, "I am excommunicated." He placed his hands gently on my head and prayed in words I had never heard before. I **instantaneously** stopped sobbing and as Father prayed in those strange words, I was being filled with a peace that went beyond all understanding. I **know** the Lord was calling me back to Himself. He didn't want fear to keep us apart. He wanted me to take my eyes off of myself and place them on Him. Once I did that, I felt the love of God flood my soul. His forgiving love **washed me** through my own tears. His healing touch, through the laying on of Father Ken's hands, brought me a peace that has **never** left me!

That was on a Thursday night in October. That Saturday, my mother returned to the Church and the Sacraments, never to miss Mass again. I'll never forget the look on her face when she came out of the confessional. She looked like a **child** that was just given the desire of her heart. She told me, as I sat quietly beside her, that it was the first time in over twenty years she had been to confession. Her beautiful eyes glistened with tears as she said, "I thought Father Ken forgot to give me a penance. When I asked him for one, he told me, 'You have lived it for twenty years. Now, all the angels in heaven rejoice, Kitty. Go in the peace of Christ and pray for me'." I was overwhelmed with love for her. To **me** she had **always** been a living saint. She had such a deep faith in God that no matter what happened in life, somehow God always worked it out. She spoke so lovingly about Mary, the Mother of God, that I was sure she knew her personally.

I never really understood why my mother didn't go to Mass **with** us while we were growing up and yet made sure my brothers and I went. I wondered, now, why she had waited so long when her love of God had always been so strong. Looking at her, I realized that God **alone knows** each of us better than we know ourselves. He **alone** searches the hearts and minds of all his children and He **alone** "understands" and accepts us just the way we are. More importantly, He **loves** us into wholeness. All of a sudden, **why** she had been away was no longer important to me. What **was** important, was the fact that each of us had come back to Him with all our hearts, in our **own** way, and the Lord was there to embrace **each of us** and clothe us in the splendor of His **unconditional** love.

I'm sure you **guessed** by now, that we **did** continue through the Seminars. We had the "laying on of hands," as it is called, to **release** the **power** of the Holy Spirit that was in us since Baptism and Confirmation. During my Baptism, my **godparents** said I would accept "Jesus Christ" as my Lord and Savior. During my Confirmation I was called to be a **witness**. But, how do you **witness** to someone you really don't **know**, only believe in? I was about to find out! Now **I** would not only invite Him into my life, but **I, myself** would ask Him to be my Lord and Savior. I told Him I wanted to **use** the power of the Holy Spirit that was given to me so that I could grow into what He wanted me to be. I **asked** Him to **empower** me, as He did His apostles, so that I could go out into the world and tell everyone that He is a God of the **living**, not of the dead.

These words were prophesied over me: "Listen to this word and **hear** it. I have given you the gift of faith and with others you must share it." I have tried to do just that, ever since, not only by my words, but by my actions. I want everyone to **see** Christ **living** in me, so they too will **know** He lives! When anyone is drawn to me, I **know** it is the Christ **in** me they are drawn to, for apart from Him I can bear **no** fruit that will **last**. But when I am **rooted** in Christ, "the tree of life," I just **naturally** bear the fruits of His Spirit. The fruits of the Holy Spirit, according to scripture, are: love, joy, peace, patient endurance, kindness, generosity and faith—regardless of the

circumstances in our lives. This can only come about through His power at work in us. Through the power of His Spirit at work in **you**, He can do more than you could **ever** possibly **imagine**. Can He give you more meaning in your life? . . Yes! Can he heal you in mind, body or spirit? . . Yes! Can He deliver you from despair, anger, resentment or jealousy? . . Yes! Will He take away all your problems? . . Maybe and maybe not. He **will** give you, the grace, strength and courage needed to deal with every situation, through the power of His Spirit at work in you.

This gift of the Holy Spirit in your life will bring about a sense of overall well being and a new freedom of self. Many times we fear change; we don't want to **"be"** different, we only want **things** to be different in our lives. I can **assure** you, God doesn't **change** us. You **"become"** a new creation—very much like the butterfly coming out of the cocoon, still a **butterfly**, but with a new beauty and **glorious freedom**—free to be you.

IF THE SON FREES YOU, YOU WILL TRULY BE FREE

John: 8,36

When I was a child, I thought like a child, I acted like a child, I even played with childish things. Although I grew in wisdom and age, the **child** within me remained.

The Lord allowed me to understand that the child within **each** of us must be healed in order for us to be **whole**. Speaking to my heart, He said, *"I know every heartache you've ever had. I've seen every tear you have ever shed. I want to heal you from the effect of all the wounds and scars you have ever suffered."*

I started recalling things in my childhood—different memories and the feelings associated with each of those memories—incidents I thought long forgotten and very insignificant.

Sharing an incident with you may help you to understand, because it is difficult to explain. I totally recalled myself in an experience at the age of twelve. I saw my teacher call me up in front of the class. She told me I should be ashamed of myself for wearing a nylon blouse that everyone could see through. I was told to go home at once and to return, dressed properly. This memory was so vivid, I could **feel** my shame rushing through my red face. I remember running out, tears streaming down my cheeks, running, running to my home, safe at last in the arms of my mother. After relating everything, she said, "Stop crying, there is nothing to cry about." "Nothing to cry about! I'm dying inside." I wanted to scream, "What do you mean there's nothing to cry about?" I changed, as she told me to, and back to school we went, she angry and wanting to give the teacher "what for" and me **dreading** every single step of the way. Once back at school, she addressed the teacher, "Didn't you think of this child's feelings? Kathy ran into the house crying, she was so embarrassed. You should be ashamed of **yourself**. I'm the one who puts her clothes out each morning; she's only a child." After my mother left, I sat down, convinced everyone was laughing at me or feeling sorry for me, depending on the type of person they were. Instantly, like a replay, the memory flashed again. Something beautiful happened. "Jesus" entered the **moment** I felt that **shame**. He comforted me, held me, said He **knew** everything I was feeling and He **understood** my pain. I **knew** the child within was completely healed of that experience.

On another occasion, I remember thinking what a shame it was that I had such a poor relationship with my father. Feeling really good about **my** relationship with the Lord, I thought I would pray for **my father**. I asked the Lord to heal my father, to **open his eyes** and **heal his heart**. I prayed that He would allow my father to see the pain within my mother, brothers and me. I prayed, "Please Lord, open **his** eyes and heal **his** heart." Deep within my heart, He spoke, "Kathleen, how about I open **your** eyes and heal **your** heart." He allowed me to see all the anger and resentment I had felt towards my father. How destructive those feelings were to me. They weren't hurting my dad; he wasn't even aware of those feelings. God allowed me to see my father, with all **his** hurts, all **his** broken dreams. Suddenly, I saw the little boy within Him, the little boy whose father had walked out on him. A little boy who never heard his father tell him how much he loved him or how special he was. A flood of emotion swept over me, and a deep love welled up within me and washed all the resentment away. I knew, if I had "Jesus" **within me**, I had to allow His love to **flow out** to others. I sat down and wrote my father a letter, telling him how God had touched my life. I told him I was sorry for all the years we wasted and hoped that in the years ahead we could enjoy and appreciate each other. I told my father I loved him. I asked him to forgive **me**, as I had forgiven **him**, as God had forgiven **both** of us. I praise and thank God for the gift of His Spirit, for all the ways He has touched my life with His healing love.

Once God opened my eyes and healed my heart, I acquired a **new spiritual way** of thinking. I started to see my father **differently**, as though I had received **corrective lenses**. When the Lord removed the bitterness and resentment from my heart, He gave the gifts of love and compassion in their place. God, in His Wisdom, never leaves a **void** within us. He never takes anything **from us**, without giving a **gift** in return.

God has called us to love others **as** He has loved us. He has loved **me** as I **am**, with all **my** weaknesses, with all **my** faults. Now, I try to love **others** as He has loved **me. I ask** that **I** may see others as He sees them. I ask that I may **decrease** and He may **increase** within me, so that I **can** live on in **His love.** I find the more I open myself to the love of God, the more free I am to be myself.

THE SPIRIT OF TRUTH

The Paraclete, the Holy Spirit whom the Father will send
in my name, will instruct you in everything, and remind
you of all that I told you.   John 14, 26.

His word says He will give His Holy Spirit to all who
ask. Why don't **you** ask Him today?

Many times we say, "I don't need that! I am a good
person, I love my family, I try to live a good life." That's a
lie of the most subtle kind. In believing that lie, we settle
for less of ourselves, we settle for less in our lives.

Often times we go through our spiritual lives the way
children go through school, thinking they are **good
enough**, they don't need to study. Isn't that what we do
with God?

I recently spoke to a woman in the parish about
coming to a prayer meeting. "Oh," she said, "I don't need

that. I'm a good Christian. I think it's wonderful for those who need it though." Three weeks later, I stopped by her house to pick something up and as we chatted, her young son came into the room. One look at his face and I knew he had done something wrong. "Hurry, I opened the refrigerator and a gallon of milk fell out. It's all over the floor." The mother ran into the kitchen and this is what I heard: "You're so stupid. Why didn't you grab it before it fell. You can't do anything right. Get out of here, I'll clean it up." A loving mother, but not an "A" mother. None of us is. I praise God I can recognize I'm one of those who need "that." "That" being the power of the Holy Spirit in my life to help me become a better wife, mother and child of God. My husband Ed and I go to a prayer meeting each week, whether convenient or inconvenient. As a result, our love and respect for one another have grown deeper every day.

The prayer meeting offers a beautiful opportunity to come together in the unity of the Holy Spirit, to praise and thank God for His love and His mercy. As we gather together, we thank Him for all the many ways He has blessed us. We thank Him for loving us just the way we are, with all our faults, with all our failings, with all our

imperfections. We lift our voices to Him in song and He, in His love, ministers to each of **us** through the music. What a wonderful God we have!

When we read His holy word, He washes us clean and bathes us in His healing love. His word **is** living and effective, so it cuts through our inmost being, correcting, encouraging, setting us free from anything that would hold us bound or stifle the Spirit of God at work in us. He is Mighty God!

He speaks the **loudest** in the **silence** of our hearts, while we sit in His **presence.** His word gives us **courage, grace** and **strength** for each day. Words of **wisdom, knowledge** and **discernment** come forth, giving us **direction** and **guidance.** He lovingly tells us how **special** each of us is, how wonderfully He made us in His own likeness and image. He encourages us to be patient with ourselves and each other, that we may **grow** into the fullness of Christ Himself, through the **power** of His Holy Spirit at work in us, doing **more** than we could ever possibly imagine.

Hearing His word deepens our faith and **enables** us to bring our petitions to Him. We lift our loved ones to Him and ask God to minister to each one according to their needs. We offer Him the **desires of our hearts** and trust in His love and mercy to hear and answer us. We close each prayer meeting as we began, united in one heart, one mind, one Spirit, as we say, "Our Father, who art in heaven, hallowed be Thy name. Thy Kingdom come, Thy will be done, on earth as it is in heaven." This prayer meeting is not a cure-all, it is not a magic hour. But it is, truly, a **holy hour.**

I share this with you to help you understand that any time we reach out to touch God, He is there! He has **no** favorites; He loves each and every one of us as though there were only **one** of us to love. He doesn't call those who are anointed and blessed; he blesses and anoints all those He calls. And, He calls **all** of us. He calls to all His children throughout the world, Jew and Muslim, Christian, atheist and gnostic, no matter the creed or race. We are His! *"Come to me all of you who find life burdensome and I will give you rest."* God wants **all** of us to rest in Him. He wants **all** of us to move and have our being in Him. "There is **one** Lord, **one** faith, **one** baptism; there is **one** God and Father of **all** mankind, who is Lord of **all,** works through **all,** and is **in all.**" Eph. 4, 5-6.

You, too, are **one** of His children. Call to Him, wherever you are, whatever you are doing. No answering machine, He'll answer everyone personally! His holy word tells us: *"Thus says the Lord, who made the earth and gave it form and firmness, whose name is Lord, 'Call to me and I will answer you. I will tell to you things great beyond reach of your knowledge.'"* Jeramiah 33, 2-3.

I have walked with the Lord for twenty years now; yet compared to the agelessness of God, I will **forever** be **learning** and **growing** in the **knowledge** and **love** of God.

Just as babies, under the protective eye of their parents, learn to crawl, sit up and eventually walk, so too it is with the children of God, as they grow in the spirit of His love. He allows us as much **independence** as we need, but being children, when He gives us an inch, we take a mile and usually wind up in trouble. He waits until we cry out, all the while never taking His eye off us. He calls to us by **name**, but again we choose to ignore Him. Sometimes we realize our need for Him quickly and reach out for His helping hand. Other times we keep trying to do it ourselves. We keep stumbling and falling and finally, exhausted and spent from trying to do our own thing in our own way, we **surrender**! He comforts and consoles us, dries our tears, heals our heart and binds up our wounds. He holds us close to His Sacred Heart and the fire of His own divine love ignites a fire within each of us. That's what the **Baptism of the Spirit** is. Scripture tells us, "Jesus" came to set a fire upon the earth. He wishes the fire to be ablaze in **each** of us. Just as a fire consumes and radiates, so too, the Spirit of God within each of us **consumes** our own sinfulness into His love which **radiates** out of us. The more we open ourselves to God, the **less sinful** we become. When we look at a fire ablaze in a charcoal pit, we notice the black coals become **white** as the fire **consumes** them. Something **similar** takes place within our own souls—we **become** pure of heart. It doesn't happen all at once; it happens **day by day**. Each day is an **opportunity** to see God more clearly in the events of our everyday lives, to **recognize** Him in every joy and every sorrow.

I wrote the following prayer many years ago as I became aware of His **presence** with me at **every moment**.

"Lord, give me the grace not to look
to the past, for I would truly boast of how
far I have come. Give me the grace not to
look to the future, for I would tremble at

how far I have yet to go. Please give me
the grace to see you in the **present
moment**, for that is where we **are**."
I began to understand that when I looked to **yesterday**, it
was gone. When I looked to **tomorrow**, it was uncertain.
But **today**, right **now**, I am here, in peace and security,
because God is **with me**.

He would have us know that everything that happens
to us in this world is **temporary**. It will pass. Our joys and
sorrows, our wealth or poverty, it will all pass away. His
word alone, will not pass away. He **hides** that word in our
hearts. When we need **hope, courage** or **love** in times of
despair, fear or **loneliness**, we need only turn our
thoughts to Him. His word goes **forth** and it will
accomplish the work for which it was **sent** to do. Anxiety
will be replaced by **peace**. We will receive **comfort** to
dispel loneliness. Fear will give way to **courage**. Where
there is animosity and hatred, **forgiveness will prevail**.
God **alone** is the very **source** and **supplier** of all our needs.
He will **minister** to each of us according to our own
individual needs. Does that mean we will get everything
we **want**? No! It means that He will give us everything
we **need** for our **own** salvation. He really did come to

save us—save us from our sins, save us in spite of ourselves. One of the greatest scriptures I have ever read is this: "What profit does a man show who **gains** the **whole world** and **destroys** himself in the process? What can a man offer in exchange for his **life**?" Mark. 8, 36-37.

How are you doing in **your** life? Who and what is the center of your life? When your life is over, what do you think will happen to you and all those you love? Are you comfortable with your answers? If you're really not sure, then call to the Lord and He will answer you. He will tell you things great beyond your knowledge. He will enlighten your mind and understanding into the mysteries of God. You will begin to appraise things in a new, spiritual way of thinking. Your life and your world will have new meaning.

I can tell you, from my own experience, that every aspect of my life took on new meaning. I began to see my role as a wife and mother with a new perspective. I started to realize in a relatively short time, that the Lord took my good marriage and made it better, stronger, deeper. All marriages are not without problems. When two people **commit** themselves to one another **forever** and live out that commitment, side by side, day by day, of course problems will exist. What we need is **grace** to overcome those problems, grace to see each other through God's eyes. Then and only then can we love as He loves. No longer are we hurt as easily by our mate's words or actions. Nor do we hurt our mates as easily by our words or actions. Love **responds** to love. As I started to decrease and Christ started to increase within me, I became more loving and compassionate, much more understanding and definitely less self centered. In trying to meet my husband's needs (not wants), my own needs were being fulfilled. Something very beautiful began to happen. Our children were responding to the sense of unity in our home. They became much more tolerant and understanding with one another. The children had always loved each other. Now, they appreciated each other. A subtle change, yet everyone was aware of it. To this day, they are each others' best friends. What a gift!

I always considered myself a good mother—one who loved her children deeply and tried to give them **everything** they needed. Not until **I** accepted the Lord into my life, did I realize I had failed to give them the **only** thing they needed, "Christ." Oh, they all went to Church and those of age went to Catholic school. They **believed** in

God, but they really didn't **know** God. They thought God was in the priests, the nuns, ministers or Rabbis, yet they never saw God in **themselves.** Once I became aware of God's presence in **my** life, I was able to **show** them the presence of God in **their** lives. Their belief in God, their **head** knowledge, if you will, became **heart** knowledge when they **experienced** God's presence in their own lives.

That's how it is with all of us. We have to **recognize** the Lord in **ourselves** before we can **recognize** Him in **others.** To **recognize** someone you have to **know** who they **are.** "Hi , God, it's me, Kathleen." I **know** Him and He **knows** me. I had to **experience** His life **in me** to **know** him and to **show** Him to others. I could effectively **witness** to the Lord once I realized he **lived** in me! **Now, I** can go forth in the boldness of His Holy Spirit. Now, I can yield to His life within me, His power at work, **in me.**

I always **believed** in God. I **saw** Him in others, I **heard** His word. I was **taught** the truths about Him through the Church. My parents talked to me about a loving God. I believed, by **faith** I believed! I just never believed He was **alive in me.** Or should I say that I never really looked for Him **within.** Never forget that the kingdom of God is within you.

YOUR LIGHT MUST SHINE AMONG MEN
Matthew 5,16.

God is all Goodness! When we are drawn to someone who is loving and kind, we are really being attracted to the Christ within them, because God is love. God's love shines through us. That's why He tells us, "You are the light of the world."

So often I hear, "Where's this world going?" With all the vice, violence, poverty, pornography and the like, you really do have to wonder. The world is going to hell, don't let it take you with it. By that I mean, don't **give in** to the ways of the world. Instead, **give up** all the things that would take you away from God. Don't become brainwashed by television, which would lead us to believe that it is only natural to sleep around, to have adulterous affairs and to be sexually active as a teenager. Is this really the thinking of our society today?

We have allowed and accepted blatant sexuality, violence, homosexuality and the like into our homes, day in and day out. Our young, innocent children are being **programed** for immorality. The commercials and advertisements are selling sex, pure and simple. How many times have you heard it said that the young men and women today have **little or no** moral values? My answer is, "Have we shown them strong moral character by our **example** or **conversation?** Or has television and peer pressure given them their values?" We must let our light shine among men and women and children everywhere. What happens when you walk into a darkened room? You stumble and grope around. But, when someone turns the light on, the darkness is gone and we are confidant and sure footed. The very same will take place in our lives and in the lives of others. We all have the light within us, but not all of us have plugged into the power. The source of that power is the Holy Spirit in our lives.

What do you **think** the **role** of the Third Person of the Trinity is? Maybe you've never thought about the Holy Spirit at all, let alone His role in our lives. The Holy Spirit enlightens our minds and understanding to accept the truths that will bring us to our own salvation. We begin to see in a new way, all the things in our lives that would **stifle** the Spirit of God at work in us. Sometimes there are great obstacles, sometimes small obstacles. But, through the power of His Holy Spirit, darkness gives way to light. His Spirit in us begins to wash us clean, so that it becomes **obvious** to us when we are smudged by sin. We can plainly see it and go **immediately** to the Lord, confess it and ask Him for His forgiveness.

I have a white curtain on the window of our front door. Having a large family, the front door is exposed to a lot of traffic. Sometimes I don't realize how dingy and dirty it becomes. Not until I wash it clean and hang it back up, do I **realize** the **state** it was in. Once clean and white, it is very easy to **see** any soil or stain on it. That is when I **should** take it down and clean it—right away. That's how sin **affects us** in our lives. A little smudge here, a little dirt there—not too bad. Only, after awhile, we too become dingy and we don't even **realize** it. You know, it's not the big black spots—we try to avoid the **big** sins—it's the subtle little ones, that dull our consciences. Then we can't **realize** the state of our own souls. How is the state of your soul, truthfully? White, full of grace, dingy or maybe even dirty? Go to the Lord, **whatever** state you're in, and you will find grace, forgiveness and healing, even deliverance. He will supply whatever you need, so that, "**your** light will shine among men."

Have you ever noticed that the light in people considered to be holy can and does dispel the darkness in others? The bad language or dirty jokes are not voiced in their presence. Whenever someone does so, they always say, "Sorry, I didn't mean that." Could you imagine someone showing Pope John Paul II pornography or telling him a dirty joke? No, because they respect the "Spirit of God in him." So, actually, the Spirit of God is **convicting** them. Notice I say convicting, **not** condemning. He is shedding His light in the darkness of our lives every day—through one another, through His Holy Word, the Bible, through Mass and His precious body and blood, through the religious services and ministers that are committed to the Lord. Will you let your light shine? A **little** light can dispel the **darkness** in a **large** room. What do you think would happen in our world, if **everyone's** light were shinning?

The Father **sent** His light **into the world** through His Son. The Son **sent** His Spirit **into the world** through us.

Now the Spirit **sends** us **into the world** through each other.

I'm sure many of you entertain doubts! You're in good company; many of the first disciples did too. I ask "Jesus" to address those doubts, now, as He did then, through His word:

> *Full authority has been given to Me both in heaven and on earth.*
>
> *Go, therefore, and make disciples of all the nations . . .*
>
> *Baptize them in the Name of the Father, and of the Son, and of the Holy Spirit.*
>
> *Teach them to carry out everything I have commanded you.*
>
> *And know that I am with you always until the end of the world.*

What the world needs now is

God.

AXIOMS and QUOTES
by KATHLEEN STOTSENBURGH

"Because we are the salt of the earth, we should season everyone we meet, so they will thirst for the Living Waters."

"I believe God often pulls the rug out from under us so that we will fall on our knees."

"Forgiveness is the 'Silent Embrace of Love'."

"God's inexhaustible *Grace* puts a song in my heart and a smile on my face."

"Jesus' broken body was taken down from the cross and laid in the arms of His Mother; so too, today, the broken body of Christ (His Church) should be placed in the arms of His Mother and remain there until He comes in Glory."

"The more we avail ourselves to the power of God, the more power of God we will have available."

"To live in the *present moment*, means to live in the *presence* of God, that we may receive grace for *each* moment."

"My words and actions, response or reactions no longer depend on others; I am free to be me."

"Signs will accompany believers, but the "extraordinary sign" is when we love others as God loves us; then all will come to believe."

"To be mindful of *our* faults is *not* to be mindful of other's."

"If we stay *rooted* in the tree of life, we will just *naturally* bear the fruit."

"To depend *completely* on God allows me to be *completely free.*"

"As I surrender my life into *His hands*, He fashions me into *His* likeness and image."

"If there is no *surrender*, there is no growing into the fullness of Christ."

"We learn from *experience*; that is *why* I place my trust in God."

"If I can not witness to God's love, then I am *not* living a life born of His Spirit."

"When *we* reach out to touch God, it is *He* who leaves His imprint on us."

"The only way to prevent burning is to constantly *bask* in the *Son*."

"We must go beyond responding to God's will and *act* on it—Gethsemane plus Crucifixion."